I Know You

by Alice Bergin

Alice's Angels
Publishing

I Know You

First published in Great Britain in 1999 by Alice's Angels Publishing
4 Lynwood Avenue, Lowton, Warrington, Cheshire. WA3 1HJ

ISBN 0 9536463 0 0

Printed in England by Gemini Print 01942 712480

Alice's Angels
Publishing

This book is dedicated to the angels,
in appreciation
of their beautiful work.

I Know You

I know you.
You were there when I was born.
You were there when I died.

You were there when the world was lonely.
You were there when I needed comfort for my soul.

You were there when I loved you,
There for every moment of this journey.
You were there when it hurt to live,
There when I longed to give,
There for the grief and the joy.

I know you.

Talk to Me

Talk to Me in the silence of your heart.
Leave the noise and anxiety of your day
To wander peacefully in the garden I have prepared for you.

Talk to Me in the serenity of your soul.
Cease the struggle to understand with your mind
And journey trustingly into the Unknown where you are known forever.

Talk to Me in the honesty of your unbelief,
Allowing questions to lead you ever deeper into My Truth.
Wear then, with unique footsteps, your own path home...

My path for you of Love.

Holy Love

In darkness,
Where designs create the vivid images.
In desire,
Where sorrow is the buried treasure.
In asking,
Where the answer confuses the question.
There is Holy Love
But here is thrice denial.

In silence,
Where the harmony of voices attains perfection.
In serenity,
Where the swan transcends the crystal waters.
In tears,
Where the mist caresses the hollows.
There is Holy Love.
Here is the answer to your question,
The question you need never ask.

See How I Love You

When the dawn comes darkly
To cast its shadows on another lonely landscape
Don't think too harshly of me
For you must know I love you.

Don't let the watery sun blind you
To the sparkle of the morning mist
As it hovers over web and dew
Calming your world with gentleness.

Don't let the cold and devious voices deafen you
To the glorious silence of honest Love
As it caresses your memory
And gives birth to a new and deeper Love tomorrow.

ॐ

Know Me. I Am Within You.

Know me.

I am within you.

Feel My presence

Notice My hand in your life.

Do not walk into the cold grey mist

Of loneliness, despair, self-doubt and isolation.

But come again into the warmth, the glory of the Light.

And share what you know.

Know Me.

I am within you.

Always

In the loudest crowd
I am there
Strong and silently reassuring.

In the loneliest landscape
I am there
Companionable and quietly comforting.

On the coldest winter's day
I am there
Warm as a Christmas fireside.

In the bleakest heart
I am there
True, open and kind.

In the darkest hour
I am there
Light of lights.

If you ask where am I
I am there
I am here.

I am Love
I am Peace
I am Yours
Always.

Love's Gentle Unfolding

Reaching beyond the known is the struggle of the intellect to grow and to progress,
seeking vainly to walk with other pilgrims on the path.

To release this striving and allow the Divine to unfold in God's time is the art,
the humility of life.

To stay still, not even waiting or hoping, provides the peaceable way for
Truth to find you and express itself to and through you.

It is not in your doing that you are manifest. It is in your being.

It is who you are when you consciously unmask,
removing the layers of personality and revealing the vulnerable light within.

Your beauty is that you are a unique fragment of God,
reflecting God's light back to Him with clarity and joy.

Alone or all one, each fragment contains the whole Truth
and the whole Truth contains each fragment.

Cease to run away into your beliefs about sinful darkness and live out in the light of Love.

Fear will not hide you forever. It is merely an avoidance.
How easily pride misleads you. How kindly Love guides and corrects,
bringing you out of your confusion and safely home.

Beloved

If, in my mind,
I feel betrayed by my family,
Mocked by my friends
And stoned by strangers,
In my mind,
I grow afraid to speak my Truth freely.

While, all the time, in my Soul,
I am beloved.
Together, it is safe,
Through all Eternity
To be free.

And, in this awareness, I see that
My family, friends and strangers
Are beloved too.
We are each others' guides to freedom.
We remind each other to call home often
For lessons in trust, humility and love.

We are all free
To be
Betrayed and betrayer
Mocked and mocking
Executed and executioner.

If, in my mind,
We are separate,
I am alone.

But because, in our Souls,
We are beloved,
We are all One,
We are free.

Your Gift to Give

Radiate your love
As the sun sends golden rays
Of warmth, light and comfort,
Encouraging dry seeds
To blossom,
Closed buds
To open,
Empty hearts
To burn with a new glow of hope.

Radiate your love,
Your gifts, unique,
Your beautifully simple wisdom.
And may the joy you share
Reach countless mirrors,
Returning home, at sunset,
To still your soul with Peace.

Out of the Depths

I hear you call me from
Down down deep
A distant murmur
Recognised by the same in me
As I created in you.

This is a call I answer
A painful cry of knowing me
But being unable to find me.
I hear. I see. I feel. I am.
I know you.
I am you.

Flying Free

There are feelings that reach out softly
To bring a contented, enveloping warmth,
Feelings that shiver and thrill
Denying will and reason
With their fleeting glimpse of some other place.

There are feelings that sparkle in memory
As the diamonds sprinkled, unattainably
Over misty English meadows.
And there are feelings
Desolate, alone, wearying and sleepless
That turn nimble feet to solid rock.
That cage a living spirit
And keep a soul in secret shadows.

Wherever feelings flirt with our fragility
There is ever the hope of a new dawn arising,
Sweetly born in the gentle faith
That always returns, albeit by surprise,
The feeling that is, that was, that will reassuringly be
The feeling of flying free.

The Angel of Passing

Before we die, the beautiful Angel of Passing comes and introduces herself to us,
so we are not afraid of her when it comes time to travel.

She hovers around and checks the little details.

She reminds the carer to plump the pillow and warm the soup just enough.
She prompts us to straighten a night-gown when it is tangled and restrictive.
She holds a lonely, cold hand and comforts a tired, cramped foot.

She re-plays a lifetime in an instant.
She slows sudden chaos and catastrophe to absolute stillness,
providing endless time to reflect.

She sits calmly by, transforming human crisis to heavenly harmony.

And she brings God's Love, so the passing is only familiar and without fear.

See her in the doorway.

This angel is Love.

She exists for everyone dying.

So no-one ever dies alone.

The Deep Within

Deep within I know Truth.
Deep within I have a code of conduct.
Deep within I find help, advice and loving guidance.
Deep within there is all I need.

So what am I doing out here
But surviving like a
Fish out of water...
Precariously,
Blithely, yet
Hopelessly stranded?

Help me back to the
Ocean of Your Love
The Deep Within.

Not I But You.

Try to be perfect ?   Not I.

Seek for Salvation?   Not I.

Look for Love?   Not I.

Listen for concurrence?   Not I.

Strive for success?   Not I.

Make it happen?   Not I.

Fight for justice?   Not I.

Right wrongs?   Not I.

Teach and preach?   Not I.

When any 'good' is to be done,
Let it not be I but You.
For then there is not judgment
Then there is only You

What need I
When all is You?
No need at all.

A Word of Comfort

When you have let yourself down and
Undone every last thread of the
Tapestry you so lovingly wove,
Where may you turn to find comfort?

When you have cast the long shadow of
Judgment over a place
You believed to be Love,
What wisdom can light that darkness?

When serenity seems a long lost myth,
When Truth's ideals are compromised
By the cacophony of bitterness, anger or pain,
There is nowhere to turn.

But to you.
In hope.
Inside.

༜

Simply Yourself

If you want to know your soul, forget who you think you are and what you think you know.
Just be, instead, in the glorious silence, the beautiful presence of your self -
the you you have always been and will always be.

In here, is your Being, your connectedness, your Divinity.
In here, you exquisitely touch and are touched beyond feeling,
beyond sensory delight, in realms of inexplicable loveliness.

Let go your quest, your search for the spiritual path, your concepts of journeying,
exploring, realisation, actualisation...

You complicate the sublimely simple with your ego's cravings.

You have nowhere to go, to travel, to find, to explore.
You are here, now, in the truth you never left.
Open your eyes and your heart.
You are home.

❧

The Refuge

I raised my heart above the clouds, above the sun
And rested there in unseen realms,
All earthly cares left way below.

How sad the troubled mind that does not know this place
Or flee to it for comfort..

For all our small, inconsequential fretting,
There is a salve, a blessed retreat,
Just above the level of the lowered eye of desolation.

Look up, in faith,
With trust in all that is unseen
And know the place of hopefulness
Where souls let go of grounded woes
And fly...
Supported by the very breath of God.

Be Still

Be still.

Turn your mind from
Grasping, seeking, needing and wanting.
Rest, instead, in this moment of clarity,
Sure, safe and silently heard.
Here, even your most secret yearning is satisfied
When only you give up the quest.

Be still.

Let thoughts play around you
Like so many falling leaves.

Stay still.

And life becomes an effortless dance
Whisking away
Old broken habits of
Worry and demand, judgment and suffering.

Be still
And award yourself, your soul to the sky.

Therefore

I think, therefore I ache.

I judge, therefore I suffer.

I fear, therefore I stagnate.

I love therefore.

❧

Friend & Companion

Who are you that you would accompany me on this, the path of life?

Who am I that I would seek your company?

Who are we, in togetherness,
Strangers, claiming to love each other?

Who has the Knowing to make this connection
For our mutual learning?
And who will be there when we fall, again?

It is All You.
So why worry?
Our lives are not only in safe hands...
They are safe hands.

❧

The Whispered Word

From beyond the limits of what I thought I knew,
Truth came strolling in,
Light and laughing,
Sprinkling the wonder of her wisdom
On two who needed to meet each other again.
"See," she said, "how right we are together."
"Feel," she smiled, "the tenderness we share."
"Touch," she gentled, "the nature of your being."
"Know that we are One."

"Skip along with me," she called.
"Catch me, hold me, keep me in your care.
Treasure me in your heart and I shall never seek to leave.
I am the whispered word, the instinctive guide,
The knowing you have in stillness.
Stay near to me,
Come home with me,
For I am you as you dream of being.
I hold the promise of our togetherness.
Run with the wind.
Be free as I tease you on.
But know, however hard you chase,
I am within.
I am forever."

Departures

Where are you going on this beautifully rainy day,
now that you've planned your schedule
to earn your keep
tidy your home
organise your meetings,
travel about full of aim and objective?

Where are you going
and what will you be when you get there?

☙

Change

Cygnet to swan.
Caterpillar to butterfly.
Me to You.

෨

The Light

Stark, electric power lines streaked from sea to sky,
connecting realms of earth and heaven with surges of enlightenment.
In the flash, all was there to be seen -
clear, illumined, bright, divinely majestic.

Expressing joy beyond the mind's admission,
laughter giggled in harmony with the ocean's lively dance.
Cool breezes washed through the heavy air and, with them,
a different silence.
Not the eerie, mysterious stillness of moments just gone,
but a calm, clear, blue-tasting freshness,
clean like a great mistake forgiven.

The thunder, its work complete, rolled inexorably on
in vast and heady magnificence, leaving behind a new song:

Know that you are as a spark of the Light,
As an image of the Limitless Energy.
Take in my power and, with every outward breath,
Illumine my Creation.
Hear the infinity of eternal knowing and, as you know me,
Speak boldly.
For then, you too are the Light, the Hope, the Message, the Truth.
What are you for but to know the Knowing,
To connect willingly with the Love, the All, your home.

Infinity

Empty silent infinite space
Allow me to enter the safe warmth of your love.

Surround me with the
Serene presence of One-ness,
The knowing that I, like you, belong,
That we are of harmony and togetherness.

In this soothing, tranquil calm,
Lead me along your divine path
To take refuge by the stream of understanding
Where all questions are answered
In joyful acceptance of what is.

Empty silent infinite space
Reveal to me the truth
And teach me to abide there always
For here, in this empty silent infinity is all I ever need.

Willingness

Exchange the arrogance of your wilfulness for the
Quiet acceptance of true willingness
And open to the lesson that is here for you.

Whatever the way, let it come.
Welcome it, knowing there are many teachers and
Countless ways all leading to one glorious awakening of the real you.

When God gives you His Truth from within your own being,
Regard its glory, its wisdom, its beauty.
And offer back only that which may be given
In curtain-less clarity - eye to eye - for how could you then refuse?

Yet you do refuse, daily,
When you let intellect overshadow with dull confusion
The perfect, visionary Light within.

Heed the messages you receive.
If you are told not to worry, then cease to worry.
Take the direction shown in its stead.
To do other is to refuse the gift of God.

What greater pain may you ever cause than
This wilful separation of saying "No" to the All
Of which you came, and are, and ever will be?

What greater disease than the sickness of turning away
from Perfect Love?

What greater sorrow than having to seek forgiveness
Of the One who only ever gave you His Peace?

Loving The Earth That Supports Us

Ever-changing hills in endless shades of subtle England green
Rolled, one on another,
Echoing the smooth curves of our planet
As she turns silently,
Entrusting her life to those she sustains.

In contemplation we saw the fragile nature
Of her glory and wondered
How to tell the forgiving field and forest,
The peaceable pasture and age-worn pebbled seashore
That we loved them.

We found our answer
Just in leaving them alone.

Lessons From The Angels

Listen and you will hear the Angels and all their helpers
who seek only to guide in their so-gentle ways.
The angels take you by the hand and they laugh
delightedly as you go willingly along the path they show you.

Angels do not tell you what to do, nor even so much as
disagree mildly with you. They simply, happily, lovingly,
acceptingly lead you to something far brighter and
more beautiful than those things you thought you knew to be true.

The Truth that angels show you is perfectly pure. It is light, bright and lovely.
You wonder whatever could have been holding you back
or what it was you were clinging to so insecurely before.

Angels understand delight - your delight as you share their delight.
We often don't understand delight but we do know it
when we experience it.
Then, we try to hold onto it and the Angels come back
to free us again from this new bond.

What a joy it is to know angelic delight and to kiss it as it passes,
trusting that a new delight will happen along -
any moment now.

Fleeting Feelings

Stand right back from your feelings and
know they are only feelings that will pass.

Listen to the inner peace, ever present in the
pandemonium out there
and be aware that no force disturbing your peace is real.

Notice the eyes you look through
for they provide the light and colour by which you see.

Exchange the judge's eyes for love's eyes
and nothing can shadow the serenity
of just gently knowing.

The Path Home

To every person a path
As purposeful as the trunk of a great oak
Reaching ever onwards for new growth and glory.

To every soul a refuge
As comforting as the shelter of an angel's wings
Where striving is replaced by peaceful home-coming.

Acknowledgements

With special thanks to Phil Askew who kindly gave permission to reproduce his photograph, illustrating "I Know You". All other photography and writing is my own original work.

Loving thanks to Ann and Geoff Napier and the dedicated team at Cygnus Book Club who helped immeasurably to make this publication possible. Thank you for your love, trust and belief. I also acknowledge with love and warmest appreciation the help and patience of everyone at Gemini Print who, with such good humour and generosity, led me through the entire design and printing process. Together, my friends, you made the impossible happen.

As always, my love and thanks to my precious parents Betty and Gerard Leeney and to my family; to blessed friends, helpers and healers: Eileen Edmondson, Julia Ramwell and Bob Powell, in memory of dear 'Natcura'; to Jim and Rosemarie Davies, Keith Summerfield; to Jeff, Tony and Philip, weavers of dreams, and to everyone I love. You know who you are.

You have been my inspiration on this incredible journey. Thank you.

Also by Alice Bergin: Just for Today, A Book of Tickets for Your Journey.

Photo by Betty Leeney